SUBURBAN
FANTASY

Michele Seminara is a poet and editor from Sydney. Her writing has twice been nominated for a Pushcart Prize and has appeared in journals such as *Cordite, Mascara Literary Review, Jacket2 Magazine* and *Australian Poetry Journal*. She has published a full-length collection, *Engraft* (Island Press, 2016), and chapbooks *Scar to Scar* (written with Robbie Coburn, PressPress, 2016) and *HUSH* (Blank Rune Press, 2017). Michele has performed her poetry, chaired panels and appeared at numerous literary events and festivals across Australia, including the Newcastle Writers Festival, Wollongong Writers Festival, Canberra Writers Festival and Queensland Poetry Festival.

SUBURBAN FANTASY

MICHELE SEMINARA

UWA PUBLISHING

First published in 2021 by
UWA Publishing
Crawley, Western Australia 6009
www.uwap.uwa.edu.au

UWAP is an imprint of UWA Publishing
a division of The University of Western Australia

ISBN: 978-1-76080-207-3

A catalogue record for this
book is available from the
National Library of Australia

Cover design by Alissa Dinallo
Typeset in Bembo by Lasertype
Printed by McPherson's Printing Group

uwapublishing

MIX
Paper from
responsible sources
FSC® C001695

Dedicated to those who by tearing me down have raised me up,
and to those who in raising me up have sustained me.

ACKNOWLEDGEMENTS

Versions of these poems first appeared in the following journals, books and anthologies: *Abridged Journal*, *Deepwater Journal*, *Bluepepper*, *Canberra Times*, *Cordite*, *Expound Magazine*, *FemAsia*; *Grieve, Volume 6* (Hunter Writers Centre); *Have Your Chill* (Donnithorne Street Press); *Hush* (Blank Rune Press), *Not Very Quiet Magazine*; *Other Terrain Journal*; *Salon Style: Fiction, Poetry & Art*; *Scar to Scar* (PressPress); *The Australian Poetry Collaboration*; *The Blue Nib*. My heartfelt thanks to the editors of these publications for supporting my work.

CONTENTS

North Facing

This house has — too many — windows:
anyone can see in.
It's one of those houses
people stroll through the back door —

they feel free.

This house was not chosen
by me but by my husband
and father who pronounced it to be
a fine, solid, master-built house
(built by masters who morph into monsters).

It opens benignly to the morning sun, turning
in the right direction (I'm told)
I should be grateful I am
not which makes me —

This house has two storeys, two stories,
the down stairs unrolling like a fiery tongue
I was always afraid to be pushed down.

But now that the opening is closing (touch wood)
I've begun to write over the holy hole
we punched in the door of hell.

(They say suffering is good for you; I can't tell.)

This is not my home. I don't live here.
I abide in the safe house my mind
has constructed from word-wood.

Only I can enter the back door:
others must knock.
If I choose not to be home, I'm not.

But here, my face faces
painfully outwards, over-
exposing its north-lit bits,
here, there is only one
room to hide in, one
secret space
in which to sit,
and this, this
gash of a poem,
this is it.

I. Blood Nature

Corinthians

Remixed from the King James Bible, 1 Corinthians 13

Love suffers
but gains nothing.
Bearer of flames, mysteries,
mountains, it rejoices
not in that which is perfect
but clangs its tongue of truth
to speak of a faith
which fruitlessly abides.

Love fails. It fails!
Seeing itself mirrored
in a childish face it is provoked
to offer its body to be burned
and always it is burned.

Love endures rudeness but longs
to be known as kindly as it knows.
And when the gift of its hope
is extinguished love seeks
cessation in the fathoms
of iniquity.

Blood Nature

After Edvard Munch's 'The Scream of Nature'

The scream punctured my sleep —
existential and unruly.
An epicentre of anxiety
radiating out to irradiate this world.

The neighbours stopped talking
to us when they heard it
my own mother stopped
answering her phone.

No one knew what to expect,
or when; the scream dictated
our heartbeats — they fled
like gods.

From the bottom of the house it rose
a siren of red up into our beds,
possessing my mouth,
the mouths of our children,
bruised blue-black from swallowing it down.

We all walked around with our gobs
ghastly wide, hands cradling dislodged minds.
Nature rebelled in familial blood
and we, in disorder, obeyed her.

I tried to smother it with love, hate, scotch,
meds, pillows. But the scream pervaded everywhere —
It spoke with tongues of fire —

I cut it free.

Family Tree

They cut the limbs off first.
Of that tree (which is me)
the one which bears
the blaring yellow x on its chest.

The arborist's eye could see
it had been wounded long ago;
then disease entered the hole at its heart
then necrosis, gliding through the vessels
in a cool grey onslaught, weakening
the branches we once festooned
for Christmas and Halloween.

Nobody noticed for a long time.
Especially, I didn't notice.
Not until the last leaves slipped
to the pavement did I look up —

They amputate the limbs
to make it easier to fell;
I know that feeling.

Now all through the house, the stench
of diesel and that terrible,
enraged squealing.

Truncated

I contemplate your arc, which has been cut.
Your projected ghost limb twitching in the glare
of my grand truncated hope.
Grief breaking bounds and bearing us
fused into myth.

Listen, I'm a mother, your mother —
It's my job to scout ahead.
Even in a world that scoffs
at maternal prescience
I persist,
baying like a bitch at spectres —
no one heeds me.

Your sight's been severed;
you can't see what I see,
the absence
of what could have been.

But you sense it, approaching,
and I watch as you race
with determination
to recalibrate
your fate.

Hush

You're bloated and there is
fear in your gaze.
You've demanded the right
to be this way and I
have acquiesced.

Mirtazapine bought no peace.

Food wrappers, razor blades, beer bottles, bong.
Your body is an energy
pushing pain into a form
which it commands the world to witness —

I witness you.

I look into your eyes and whisper
— with my eyes — I see you.

Bitch, you shoot, from the dark side of your mouth,
your head in chaotic orbit.

I'm whatever you need me to be, baby.
Let's croon the moon to sleep like we used to.

Hush.

Facetune

I crop your girth of grief
so it won't show.
Coruscate your under-eyes
in the hope that hope might grow.

Destain your teeth, raze blemishes,
out damn spot!
Blood the lips, lend bloom
to what's worn off.

I pray I could move deeper —
sweep the lungs. Restart
the heart, the mind;
unspool the past.

Return us to the prescient game
I played,
when my unconscious
conjured you this way.

Sunday Walk

The daughter's ball–hands bobble from her black
coat sleeves. Her hair
sprouts dark roots morphing to red
then cheapening to yellow.
The underbelly rises ruthlessly
out of her jeans.

I follow behind my little girl, I trail
her into the future.
And when she bounds too far
ahead, I pull
too weakly back.

It's never enough, no matter how many
times you rewind. You're still
ghosting the same tensed fists, the same
cowed back, the same determined
yet receding chin —

A Great Sorrow

It's as if a storm-grey bird
has come to roost inside you:
gravid and plump, of shifting shape,
black clacking beak, wounded
accusatory eyes.

Its weight is felt always.
Sometimes bearable,
sometimes not; but never
ceded or not yours to carry.

(Although you've come to recognise
it in the slippery gaze of others,
their sagging back-bones harbouring
engorged hearts.)

While shopping, exercising,
watching the other children play —
It curls, hard, against your ribs,
a dense and sobering canker;
your malformed babe.

Borderline

I think this is the end now,
the clearing time, the dis-engage:
disorder lay waste to my love
now love must stake her border.

My hole in bucket, hold on tight,
I — slave to salve you through the night —
your battle lines were black and white;
our family's membranes, ruptured.

The absence in your wake
takes startling shape:

ledge of loss / lump of grief
plane of despair / void of relief

shard of hope / bedevilled stairs
rend in reason / prayers like flares

swarming heartbeats / razored skin
yelp of siren / phantom limb

trailing shadow / cast-off shoe
nemesis / I got my due.

Blinds

I close the blinds to block out probing eyes.
The roses on the window sill
                                still flame against the sky.
Darkness crawls out early   from the rain.
A stranger calls   to check   that I'm alive.

Bow and Scrape

How freeing, to bow out; there's wisdom in it.
Mind's tumescence halted.
What's twisted in you
no longer twisting
in me.

Silence is best.
Stillness. Trying not
to put a word wrong.
(I speak so circumspectly these days
even the dog won't come!)

Enough. Just keep going.
(But let's admit it's not much fun.)

II. Suburban Fantasy

Suburban Fantasy

Remixed from Christina Stead's *The Man Who Loved Children*

You   maltreated

                    my poor

body

            your

     savage

         love   filling me with

child

                force-

ing

     me   down on

     your filthy

                mat-

ress

      stinking   with

            vile

     blood

  and

            roots

    you know nothing

           pack your

things   This is my house

   go

Ms. Suburbia

What a tame beast she has become, idling
in the paddocks of her family's unmade
beds and mountainous dishes

circumambulating, endlessly, the dead heart
of this domestic poppy field; pausing
with lost purpose to pick up

some   thing   here
and artfully
place   it   there —
in abstract justification
of an involutionary existence.

Look, see how she is self-
restrained by sedatives and spurred
to life by stimulants then lured
to the end of day by the promise
of the darkling hours in which to unfurl
her monstrous might and play —
(what desperate play!)

Such a noble beast is man
and such a cowed
beast is woman —
tethered by the whim
of reproduction
to her most
nominal
self.

Plot

Remixed from Philip Larkin's 'The Whitsun Weddings'

All afternoon the women shared their wounding.
Loosed from fathers, free of knots,
under their belts, the secret smut,
a hothouse lark, the race to wed,
time gripping tighter.

Along the line, children defined
the marked off landscape of their lives:
marriage struck then swelled then slowed
the girl displaced inside.

A blinding sense of nondescript,
bright parodies of dull success;
their aims like arrows falling

out of sight as if they'd died —
And not one flashed uniquely,
and nothing fresh survived.

20/20

Sixteen years ago, your mother swept past
me in the store, her eyes not dropping

to my belly. That Christmas,
we were not invited, but by the next

— granted entry after birthing their grandson —
I gifted my new parents-in-law

a free standing double picture frame:
my daughter on one side

of the divide, her baby brother on the other.
Next visit, only one of my children

buried beneath a cousin. Why didn't
I decry it then, or earlier when, the room

overblown with foreigners now called family,
your father passed his swaddled heir

around and unbound him to admire
the new jewel in his crown. Instead I chose

to push my power with all my power down.
And when the nurse asked if I was *alright, love?*

I should not have acquiesced —
for the stigma, steeped in silence, has festered ever since.

And when I saw your mother in the supermarket today,
it was I who pretended not to see.

Other Mothers

I wonder if all the other mothers'
faces pinch too —
Do they eye the time to sip respite?
Break out at night to stare longingly in?
Shock dumb limbs to life in bracing waters?

I wonder if they feed on their children /
feed their children?
If their masks itch and slip
in heat, contract
in cold; contain
the urge, the surge of
migratory flight.

If years petrify
around their sights —
the panic
of darting eyes.

If underneath their aims
are warped   like wings.

The Patriarch

If you sigh and shake
your head
I'll shame you in front of the children.

If you roll your eyes
I'll slap you sideways.

Don't imagine the money is yours:
it's never yours.
I might involve you in the decision making.

If you open your mouth
too often
you're pushing
the friendship too far.

When I want sex, you can speak.
Afterwards, shut up.

If you give me the wrong directions
I'll rip the baby from your womb.

When my father talks, you had better listen.

And so

— she exited the game, walking beyond
the bounds of retribution.

Warning — *if you say, if you say, if you say
so* — and of course he had, forcing
her mind's slide sideways.

Their life snapping shut
like a kiss lock purse.

In her wake

the memory of
an ocean.

Wax/Wane

My mother's hands
at half my age
look old when I am three.

Now tucking my child in bed
I whisper — two more minutes —
and she — three! — and then —
(sotto voce) or maybe never...

That would be nice, I agree.
Never; never leaving.

But as we wane
the full moon mocks
us all the way
till morning.

Entrapment

Between shadow and dawn
I sleep — you watch
the sky. Perception drowning
in recollection, eyes
embedded beyond.

Irises dance
amidst images,
the body a still pathway —

My untouched figure silenced
by the entrapment of your thought.

Morte Nature

After Russell Drysdale's 'Portrait of a woman'

I sit
    stolid and glowing in the gloaming.
Eyes hooked to the past.
        Painter's brush probing
my wide white collar —
    (I'll always embody more than he could imagine.)

Twelve bodies grown in mine,
            nine slipped through. Years spent
                dragging this soft anchor in the mud.

Our still lives undiminished, swelling mythic in tableau —
    I wear the proud shroud of my best blue dress.

Deconstruct

Hair
traitorous grey
shameful need to pretend anti-ageing.

Plucking / dilapidating / dyeing / dying.

Betrayal of knees, hands, feet, neck (knees?!)

circled & magnified, almost expired:
quick sale!

The male body needing no such revision.
His landscape a flagrant prairie
defining horizons, bristling grass —

La Vita Agrodolce

Foolish girl who stooped to find
redemption in her child's eye —
the young mother so assured
benign worlds would bloom there.

Now washed up on a bench
marked with plaques for the dead
— *Till love reunites us, in death, as in life* —
I reflect, with phantoms by my side,
on time's rapacious tide...

Drowning in the viscous sun,
birds swooping burning head,
thrumming ferries, lovers, dogs,
the frisson of goodbye.

(The flats where you and I once lived,
but of course, that was a lie.)

All things cleave
together; dissipate
in time.

The black crow.
The expanse of blue.
That little yellow canoe.

Graffiti

Degrade degrade degrade yourself
take care to curl up small.
Have I grown
compact enough?
Unfurl me at your peril.

In the lengthening autumn
of my shadow skirl reams of discontent —
Am I sitting meekly?
No? Forbid me speak!

Deface deface deface yourself
until you disappear.
Leave no glyphs to sign this space
(she wasn't even here).

Her heart seeks

After Emily Dickinson

Concord — first —
Then — just scope to speak —
Her words an assay into
Sovereign space

Next — licence of agency —
Then — leeway from constraint —
And finally — the absence
Of erase

III. Second Coming

In the Family

There is sickness in the family:
in the martyred mother's cervical hump
the droop of the harried father's eye
the retreat of the big sister to her bed —
(the whispers are that it's all in her head).

That the kind young nurse couldn't
stand to hold another dying
hand that Father's face is a Dali
clock palsied behind its pirate
patch that the little girl can't
come out to play because Mother's
head is bad today and how she died
while giving birth to you and her sirened spirit
only just withdrew.

So be quiet, still, and very good
this world must not be tested:
else Sister's cells will harm themselves
Father's face will elongate
Mother's fragile heart will break —
and all because of you.

Conception

I, I am the eye at the door,
with my truth-seeking mind
aloft soft foetal spine.

I slip through the slit
tumbling into space-time
where my creators
enmesh and entwine.

They are old to my young eyes
and young to my old;
unaware that our fused fate
has pre-actualised.

I raze God's plot
with my prescient gaze
and when grief ossifies
hope — I rise, I rise.

Second Coming

It seems I am the problem child, again.
Father speaking on Mother's behalf
that nitrogen cold gaze.

I bathe in it; it burns —
it always burned.
But now my skin is bound
in bitter scales.

How forlorn, to be the black one;
I don't show it.
Let them beat their breasts
and rail — I won't.

Instead, I involute, secrete this note:
beware the coming of your twice-born child.

Run Rabbit

The coiled snake
of Father's anger
sleeps at the base of his spine.

It snores through play
but rises unpredictably
to transgression.

Triggered, it shoots up and out
his customarily kind mouth.

They flee in well-versed vectors —

Run, rabbit, run!

Alas, plump and placid,
I am the slow one.

Great White Malley

Remixed from Patrick White's *Flaws in the Glass*

Beneath my mother's fur
a neo-Gothic aquarium trembled...
all blotches and dimples and ripples
and the menace of snakes.

Father was a DickyBird
who ploughed the colonial soils;
Mother took charge of the whippings —
her formidable riding-crop technique!

In the pool on steamy
mornings concealed by *monstera deliciosa*
I hung suspended
the corpse of a pale frog.
Waiting for something to happen,
something potent to pour out —
(Conscience-ridden: but what if the maid found out?)

The first erection
I remember
was the first poet I ever met.
In blank verse melodrama
Sir Topaz disembowelled his victim,
hurling 'the young man's entrails to the wind!'

God, how I relished
the smell of blood and thunder;
the aroma of saltpetre rising
from the windows of my childhood;
the purple lantana;
that magic word, EXEUNT.

A Word from the Wise Guy

Remixed from William Burroughs' *Naked Lunch*

Speaking *Personally*
(and if a man speaks
any other way shove
a pellet up his arse) beyond
a certain frequency the Sacred
is UNNECESSARY.

I have no precise memory
of the borrowed flesh
of the human form
— a condition of total exposure
tilting quixotically at *NOTHING* —
but in my psychic delirium
apparently I took notes:

Protoplasm Daddy
Step right up
and crank one in the Mother Cell;
there's room for one
more back-brain baby —
shack up at your peril!

But it's COLD OUTSIDE
and so nice-warm in here
with NAKED entities man and bestial
piled high on thermodynamic

tranquillizers, energizers, hallucinogens,
The Living Source, and my own
special cure for the hourglass run-out
a spine like Fro-Zen TIME
approaching metabolic ZERO.

Tractacus Logico-Philosophicus:
How long will this trip last?
Mutatis mutandis:
As long as we can keep it going.

So Slow-DOWN dross eaters;
no matter how
you jerk
the handle the result is —

The Harrowing

The body an inferno:

buried ancestors' voices rising
through the spire of the neck — electrifying
flesh into fire.

Captive in those human pastures
being dives into itself:
descends through binding seed,
becomes the light.

Redact

I did damage tonight —
wounded her as vaccine,
poking her in the paunch
to stave off teasing.

I'm hungry, she'd said; and all she craved
was bread.

At bedtime she cried and blamed
her brother. But I knew how
my dispatch would implode.

Who among you throws
the surest stone?

My parents left
the boys to redact me.

Did that hurt more
or less
than writing this poem?

True Crime

I've been consuming
too many crime podcasts,
have started locking the door

perceiving pervy neighbours
and opportunistic strangers
trailing silver semen on my windowsills and floor.

On Twitter, a mother marks
her daughter's inaugural public groping,
while my own child crests
the dangerous circumference of her imminent flesh —
the world pre-emptively turning to trawl
her for its pleasure and perversion.

It is a dark world in which we dare love.

Lured by the luminol glow of the lifeblood of

    Martha Moxley
Ebony Simpson
    Carly Ryan
      Tia Rigg
    Daniel Morcombe
Ana Kriégel
    Margaret and Seana Tapp

I brood deep into the murky night
over
how it's usually men who — ?
why so many women are — ?
that our forsaken children must — ?

Gum

Struggling, staggering —
your father
has cut you down.

Counting the number of feet;
a long life lodged here.

Rope, dragging, winds
inside your throat.

At the foot of the tree
for the first time
an actual Eden.

Child's Mind

Little child with eyes like darts
please hurl them at my hardened heart;
perhaps they'll lodge in fissures there
explode and blow me wild and bare.

Little child with face like corn–
field spreading far as eye can see —
allow me to drown my distress
in your anaesthetising sea.

Little child with mind like nascent
cloud on volatile day,
teach me how to dissipate
and gently fade away.

Sensate

Things are black indeed.
No! I do not wish to come.
Let the insides and the outsides rise to meet.

Shrouds of rain asphyxiate
the enshrined breath which animates;
the thunder foretells, we must be undone.

Minds twist in a tumult; sufferings compound.
Memories turn but do not liberate.

While I sit sober, still, still, and will
not yield to stir —

This clarity has been too starkly won.

Sodium Glow

The landscape of grief unfolds
miles from light.

Begging a silent god
I seek the sky;
a thrown fight.

Accelerated burial,
eyes kissed by nature's evil:
I live beside the innocent
a smoking body.

My windowless skin an
exposed   sleeping   target.

For days the drumming
of the black wind
ignites me.

memory lane

at the school reunion
I get the call
you've run
again in hospital
it seems I can't
go out without
this noose as if you

know at the school reunion
I have to ask
my old friends' names
admitting I don't
recognise
hope ossified
in layers of fat and

time at the school reunion
no chance to pee
too many stairs
don't think to check
my phone to see
your messages
of bridge and jumping

child at the school reunion
contemptuous
of other parents'
bromide woes
they'll never know
the panic
room
in the basement of my

mind at the school reunion
studying
the tranquil course
of others' lives
for clues
to how they landed
there and how I washed up

here at the school reunion
envying
the quietude of
our premature dead
a shameful truth
conceived
from scores
of little deaths
inside

The Fall

One day I shall fall
down those stairs
and it will be
a release.

As
I fall
I must surely recall
my children and taste shame.

The fall will create an elongation
in time, a lacuna for recapitulation.

And nothing will flash before my eyes —
Nothing. Only darkness; easeful darkness.

clot

sun gushing   like blood
through the grasses   water rising
like prayer   in humid air

the yard   a slow   collapse
of bone   and body   eroded by flies

fear running / headlong through a gumtree
fear thinning / peripherally in wind

fear in the barren blinkering
of a lone eye

Rope

Line cut — your dangling
words
a prayer of blessed silence

Steer clear!
all who would enter here
(portcullis closed)

You're crying out for healing
only I am means
not ends —

My glistening gut of pearls
will bind your wounds

Your silence

masses upon me;
a familiar wait/weight.
I restrain it lest it cedes and leaves
a more incisive absence.

Silence as accusation, veiled
self-violation. I try it on,
rehearsing how I might feel if —

So this is the white noise
you've always prophesised:

a resounding of renounced pain
hope   words   memory   mother.

Sirens

The reason for your silence
does not matter.

Body and breath in disconnect
as winds gather in corridors —

Screaming
was not what brought you here.

Inhabit
the urgent
anatomy of your pulse.

Retrieve what you hear inside:
the siren of voice along highways.

Counter Scars

For Robbie Coburn, remixed in response to his poem 'Scars'

the cry of my voice is enough

to collapse skin.

becoming survival
you cross   a passage
preservation wounds
forgotten.

the panic of blood
against blade along poised palm

stills.

        my breath enters

your sealed

landscapes
within.

IV. Incarnate

every morning i wake, i wake
surprised. that life appears
again with each
opening of these eyes.
that eyes arise
with opening of each day.
that when both close, all i's
fall away.

Southerly Buster

Remixed from Christina Steads' *Seven Poor Men of Sydney*

A bloody sun rose through misty veils —
another steaming white day.
Morning smoked on the red roofs swarming the hills;
the barren headland curled like a scorpion
in the blinding sea.

At the wharf, people burst
out of the turnstiles, flushed girls
in floating dresses twisting
in streams through the streets.

Cicadas skirled from the foreshores,
trees rose up to dissolve into light
and picnickers deliquesced in the cool pools
of deep green between the pines.

The afternoon, wearing on,
shone copper, the whole ocean rolling
in molten motion toward the land,
meteorologists singing up a storm
as the people, waiting, wilted.

Dusk gathered; houses shadowed.
The eight o'clock ferry trailed its golden
lights out of the wharf...
Street lamps yellowly came on —

In the gloaming, the wind charged in.

Dusty leaves twisted and blazed,
the grass reared itself with a pugnacious thrust,
rats streaked up from the waterfront,
cockroaches scuttled into cracks.

The sea was running high
gathering force in mile long rollers,
a howling parliament of waves plunging
booming into the caves then draining
hissing back off the rocks.

For hours the squall drove from the south
— battering at the window panes
chattering at the doors —
and bursts of rain rang like blasts of shot.

Then, an imperceptible illumination:
in the west, a faint low glimmer
announcing the setting of the moon;

in the east, dawn breaking through
the black clouds — the pale contour
of the heads emerging
radiant, like a somnolent lover's limbs.

Pulse

Listen now
an empty bed, the sweep
of frantic embrace.

Masked by rain you ink
your blood, your longing
an unseen formation.

This body with its shrinking
flesh, its lips   triggering words
burns closer than the darkness   beyond.

Rapture

I miss them, but it wasn't a disaster. – Elizabeth Bishop, 'One Art'

Looking through clear eyes
of imminent death, time
is a ponderous fruit
hanging heavy and swollen
with possibility
in her pendulous basket.

Globular and not-quite-ripe
she blooms with all the days
you will not see;
a still life of – fecundity squandered –
without witness, unconsumed.

God, to take just one more
bite, and this time savour
the bittersweet juices
running
down the face
and the fingers
sticky and tingling
with the messiness of it all

would be a rapture.
But – no disaster;
consciousness burgeons beyond her

disentwining from this world
despite the drive to cling and cling
and yearning for the amputated
limb of our projections, we are roused
by wise compulsion to accept life has been spent
and we must move on, relentlessly

on, without choice leaving
all those little things unsaid, undone,
without choice shedding the slithery skin
that houses us but locks us in,
and further, our very sense of selves
must fall in cascades of disguise,
unravelling us for – the chill surprise! –
of running naked, out into the rain.

Embody

This body is not a temple but a vehicle
for pleasure and pain.
This body is not a vehicle but
a manifestation of pleasure and pain.
Pleasure and pain are both sacred
and profane revelations of body.

My body swimming in water is a mere drop in a body of water.
The body of water sometimes appears as a wave.
Wave and drop are only briefly appeared
by mind's slippery karmic confluence.

When I swim with you in this precious body of seawater,
we co-create. Later, when sense perceptions urge
and attachments merge, we procreate.
Roused energies rise in steamy flesh
and ahh into the other's supple body.

Sometimes the ahh dives down like a fish and quickens into being.

Three babies have anchored in my maternal cove:
nascent body/minds blooming in mine
as I float like a yoke on the surface of
this shimmering ocean's grand dream.

Tide

Thought is longer than the night,
      the grave grey sky collapsing.
   Waves of memory dance
then die, her children
     a silent gathering —

   The sea, the sea, the sea
will drown us all.

Migraineur

recalled — by snapping synapses
in brain — to inland hushed by chemical
cascade — a swaddling rain —

migraine muscles body
to live — instead of head — in bed

and consciousness to monitor its flame.

how wise the flesh to rein the mind, to
turn its outward looking
in; re-
coil thought to meditate
the dumb pathways of pain.

vehicle tempering wayfarer —
restrain. restrain. restrain.

Uppgivenhetssyndrom

The unconscious is a precise and even pedantic symbolist.

— D. M. Thomas

All over the camps / children's eyes / revolve inwards / like moons
Their muscles wane / as minds release / cruel world

They scored their grief with razors / they lit their flesh / like flares
But now their legs lie still / as metaphor / for resignation

Behind fences / limbs grow thin / enough to slip / through loopholes
Force feeding tubes tether / life to life

Judges sanction portals / mothers' bodies flail glass
Porous eyelids gauge / time to retire

First thirst / then speech / then sight / then sense expire

Beneath the ice / you wend the blank / pathways of your mind
Your body / crossing borders / liquefied

Withdrawn / so far / so far / so far / inside

What interim world are you hiding in?
In dreams / I hear you calling / with the voice of my own child

I keep turning vacant corners / looking
For liminal beings / lost little ones / my loves

legacy

My dear, I pledge
a soft bed
to lay you down
a safe house
to harbour in
the memory of
our nighttime swims
the ogre who stalked
our fairytale walks
your painful skin
my bi-part heart
the eternal why
I couldn't satisfy
the conflicted moment
of your conception
(which must have been
when the bane slipped in)
your tiny feet
flailing even then
his broken oath
my salvaged self
our continent
now cleft in two
by aftershocks
my immutable love
a rope-ladder
to lead you
home.

Into your fair hands

Remixed from Ramon Loyola's 'A Rendering of Genes'

My

    rendering of
                 memories

       belies the notion of

An   ordinary face

    the tongue
        is   assured
              and
   eyes that defy

               sun shine
In little black corners
            of   earth

Where   light   delights

         and   hope
can only touch
   your   hands

Diminuendo

I'm learning to tread circumspectly;
my belly, soft from children,
divining the way.

Beside me the cat, utterly at ease,
and the dog's inner ears and underbelly
faithfully offered up.

I've just said prayers!
Fed flame's wrathful maul
white seed instead of black —
unprepared for this familiar, devotional urge.

The world is in tumult but in this moment
mind is still.

Do you see that cloud in the sky?
No, nor do I.

Bendalong

In Memorium B.G.T.

I wish when you came
to the cabin that morning
I'd stopped rushing and asked,
Would you like some tea?
and taken the time
to sit down with you at the long table.

It would have been fine,
just to trade idle trifles
and benignly swell our day.

You taught me how to fold
in the middle, ducking deep
down into the chill water
to explore the unplumbed world below
before leading me back
through the rising tide, scouting
a safe path to tread.

Now I hope someone shows you
how to fold in the middle;
I hope someone guides you
where to place your feet;
I hope someone helps you
to sink, without strain,
to the glittering floor of your mind.

Involuntary

An elastic covering called skin
encases our bodies, my son reads,
but I am not looking at the inlaid page
with its transparent windows transgressively
unveiling the human form's clandestine layers —

No, I am ardently watching him:
with his ripening cheeks and fecund brain
and glistening eyes of impermanence
that look to me — to me! — for solace

and tonight, as he reads, I am seeing inside
to the myriad processes functioning to hold us
implausibly within this quivering world —

and it makes my dark involuntary heart muscle shudder.

Finis

Memento semper Finis, et quia perditum non redit tempus
(Remember always your end, and that lost time does not return)

— Thomas à Kempis, *The Imitation of Christ, Book I, Chapter XXV*

For months you watched
perplexed, perhaps wondering
why we walked and played less —

or why I wept and drank
more. Then there were
those dark soul nights spent
baying in the back garden
at the stars;

the flawed organ in your vaulted
chest somehow pumping
powerfully enough to sustain us.

But as you ebbed, I failed
to notice your stiff gait,
your listlessness, the insidious
cough as your lungs began
to fill with a foamy tide.

And by the time I found
time to seek help,
you were too far gone:

your heart swamped
with human grief — unfathomable,
even for you.

Night Watch

Tonight, you escape these bones,
the body emptying of everything.

Fixed to this earth like a tongue in flesh
you cry a rain of scattered words.

Touching you, I think you are here,
eyes whispering inside silence.

Run, stranger! I am telling you —
soon you will wake

beyond nothing.

Our Land of Sorrows

History is beginning
to pool upon itself.

The length of my stare is long
enough to fracture.

Again, the map of my tongue
shrinks back to its base.

Again, the glass is clear.

Incarnate

In Memorium Ramon Loyola

I'm reading *Four Reincarnations*
by Max Ritvo, the book
an unintentional bequest
by my friend,
the poet Ramon Loyola.

Unlike Max, Ramon was evicted by his body
from life suddenly, unexpectedly.
He left like you leave
your home every morning,
intending to return.

Stepping out, his soul shed
all but what barely exits, leaving behind
just those earthly accruements which others might find useful:

a library illuminated with notes and creased corners;
his own poems — lodged like touchstones — in our minds;
the sacred relics of his recyclable organs, all
circling out there in the world of others,
a generosity of thought and flesh
reverberating through space-time.

A papery vein burst in Ramon's brain
and out tumbled his full bounty of jewels,
each orb a revelation of pomegranate seed
quickening on our tongues —
We come as supplicants, scavengers, curators,
to feast on his cryptic frieze.

And now, within the fragile bubble
of my own body/mind
as I divine Max Ritvo via Ramon Loyola,
I glimpse both poets coil
— like silver koi linked head to tail —
in the glistening chain mail of my poem.

NOTES

'Corinthians' is a found poem sourced from the King James Bible, 1 Corinthians 13

'Blood Nature' is an ekphrastic poem after Edvard Munch's painting 'The Scream of Nature', pastel on board, 1895, around the wooden frame of which is painted: 'I was walking along the road with two friends / The sun was setting – the sky turned a bloody red / And I felt a whiff of melancholy – I stood / Still, deathly tired – over the blue-black / Fjord and city hung blood and tongues of fire / My Friends walked on – I remained behind / Shivering with anxiety – I felt the great scream in nature'.

'Uppgivenhestsyndrome' is Swedish for Resignation Syndrome, a rare psychiatric condition first experienced by refugee children in Sweden and later by children detained on Nauru, who withdrew, as a result of trauma, into an unconscious state.

'Suburban Fantasy' is an erasure poem from pages 170-171 of Christina Stead's *The Man Who Loved Children*, Penguin Books, 1970.

The poems 'Entrapment', 'The Harrowing', 'Gum', 'Sodium Glow', 'Clot', 'Sirens', 'Counter-Scars', 'Tide', 'Pulse', 'Our Land of Sorrows' and 'Nightwatch' are found poems sourced and responding to poems written by Robbie Coburn. Versions of these poems first appeared in our co-written chapbook, *Scar to Scar* (PressPress, 2016).

'Morte Nature' is an ekphrastic poem after Russell Drysdale's 'Portrait of a Woman', 1945, oil on board, 61 × 51 cm.

'Plot' is a found poem sourced from 'The Whitsun Weddings' by Philip Larkin.

'A Word from the Wise Guy' is a found poem sourced from the Introduction to *Naked Lunch*, by William Burroughs.

'Great White Malley' is a found poem sourced from Patrick Whites autobiography, *Flaws in the Glass*.

'Southerly Buster' is a found poem sourced from the novel *Seven Poor Men of Sydney* by Christina Stead.

'Into your fair hands' is an erasure poem 'found' or rendered from Ramon Loyola's poem, 'A Rendering of Genes'.